UNWANTED CHILD

Unwanted Child

A Healing Memoir

CHANTAL AGAPITI

Author

Copyright © 2024 by Chantal Agapiti

All rights reserved. No part of this book may be reproduced in any manner whatsoever without written permission except in the case of brief quotations embodied in critical articles and reviews.

First Printing, 2024

CONTENTS

Prelude
1

What's In a Name?
4

Evening Confessions
7

A Lonely Child's Reality
11

A Clueless Teen's Fight
46

A Young Woman Craving Love
75

Conclusion
100

ABOUT THE AUTHOR - 105

PRELUDE

Dedicated to all trauma survivors

My body
shattered.
My mind
numb.
My soul
wounded.
Your body knows.
Your body remembers,
your soul bleeds.
The before me
gone.
The present me
awake.
The future me
hopes.

*In loving memory of my aunt,
who welcomed me with open arms
when I needed it most.
She showed me what a loving family
is supposed to look like.
She made me feel like I was a part of it
and gave me a sense of belonging.
I'll always be grateful to her for that.*

Grazie, zia.

Do you think you were born for a reason?
Do you think you were born out of love?
Do you think you were born into a loving home?
Do you exist if no one notices?

Just imagine . . .
your mom having you growing in her belly,
your mom loving you from day one,
your mom caressing her belly with love,
wanting to protect you,
wanting to be affectionate with you,
wanting to see your face,
to hold you in her arms.
Do you think this is how it was for you?
I'm so happy for you.
However, for me, I have to say
"No" to all the above.
I've always known I was an unwanted child,
and even today, as an adult, I still do.
Being unwanted doesn't end when you turn eighteen.
It sticks with you every day of your life.
Here's my story.

PLEASE NOTE I'LL BE USING FICTIONIZED NAMES TO
PROTECT PEOPLE'S PRIVACY.

WHAT'S IN A NAME?

I need a name to put on the bracelet.

"Ma'am? Ma'am? Do you have a name for this child?"

As my mother was holding her newborn baby in her arms, the midwife asked her what she wanted to name the child. When the midwife went to hand over the baby to her, the midwife repeated the question: "Ma'am, I'm sorry. I understand you're exhausted, but I need a name to put on the bracelet."

Finally, she looked over at my father without saying a word. He stared back at her, waiting for her to answer. My father was never one to take charge or control of a situation. She was always the one leading our family's decision-making, so it was no surprise that he would wait for her to decide on that occasion. But he did offer some ideas; he suggested his mother's name and the name of Italy's most renowned pizza (named after a queen), but she didn't answer. Then she asked the midwife: "What is your name?"

"Chantal," the midwife said.

My mother then told my father to use that name on

my birth certificate, and so he left for the administrative office to have them officialize it.

While he tended to that, my mother, stayed behind, healing from the natural birth she had just undergone. I was quite large for an infant, which is ironic considering I am petite-sized today. Yet back then, I weighed almost eleven pounds and was twenty inches long.

"Ma'am, I need your documents to complete the necessary paperwork."

My father hadn't returned yet, and my mother didn't quite understand what the clerk asked for. My parents moved from Italy in the mid-seventies, and she never quite learned Dutch, the language of the region they lived in. French was a lot easier for them, as Italian and French are both Latin-based languages, but Dutch was challenging, to say the least. As the administrative clerk kept insisting, she pointed a little further to her purse on the seat. The administrative clerk brought it to her, and Ursula took out her wallet and gave her ID to the clerk.

When I got pregnant, I decided what I would call my boys long before their births. Well, I decided on their names before they even came into being. That's how much being a mom and having kids meant to my husband and me. We thought about things months before, and when both were just a bundle of growing cells. So, when I found out how my parents chose my name, it was just another disillusion or confirmation about me being an unwanted child. Why else would a mom and dad not discuss, even in a playful way, what name they wanted for their child?

When you originate from the south of Italy, where

they still have strong family traditions, for instance, I have dozens of cousins with the same name, as they were named after my grandmother, and the same goes for the boys named after my grandfather. Yet, they didn't even honor that tradition. I never knew why, except for the apparent fact that I was unwanted, perhaps unworthy of carrying her parents' name.

NOTE: FROM NOW ON, I WILL REFER TO MY MOTHER AS URSULA, AS IT HURTS TOO MUCH TO CALL HER AS SUCH.

EVENING CONFESSIONS

I left home at seventeen.

When I was seventeen, just a few months before turning eighteen, I seized an opportunity to move out. I was in a relationship with someone who lived on his own, and as our relationship grew more serious, he moved into a bigger apartment. Unlike where he lived when we first met, this place was big enough for the both of us. It was September of '99 and I was about to start my senior year in high school. I just grabbed a few clothes and some personal belongings and left. My parents did not search for me or plead for me to stay home; nobody said much, actually, and neither did I.

After a while, my father showed up at my doorstep, when my boyfriend was at work, and I was home alone. He sat down on the couch and started talking. He spoke about his past and shared some new personal information about how he met Ursula and how they became a couple. At first, I was shocked by what he told me because I didn't expect him to open up like that. I didn't understand where it was coming from, and I wondered how long he'd felt the need to share this with someone. I don't know if he meant to share this with me in particular or if he just needed to, but the fact I left home brought him to me.

Once we become adults, we often think of the specific moment when we realize our parents are just flawed human beings like the rest of us. They don't have superpowers, and they're not forged to be perfect parents. They're just doing the best they can. Or at least that's what we would expect of them. This wasn't that moment for me, and I had known for a long time my parents were just swimming in the open sea, trying to keep their heads above water and not drown.

Ursula took me to handle essential errands as soon as I could read. We had no internet in the eighties, so we did our banking in person. In order to pay our bills, we had to go to the bank to make the payments. But Ursula didn't know the local language, and when they moved here in the seventies, she only spoke Italian. After a while, Ursula learned French. Learning French was more manageable for her, but Dutch was an entirely different matter.

Because of the language barrier, Ursula took me with her to explain what needed to be done to the clerk and to translate back to her what extra information the bank required. My translating duties didn't stop at the bank; I would also provide my translation services elsewhere. Sometimes, the use of words was so specific that I didn't understand it myself—for example, official governmental matters or insurance. But that was no reason to relieve me, an elementary school child, from that arduous task. No excuse was good enough, and I just had to.

During that time, it became evident that my parents

were flawed. Moreover, I felt they needed me to be more than a little child who just wanted to enjoy her innocent and playful youth. I understood I had a task to fulfill that Ursula couldn't manage. And I remember that feeling so clearly because I never stopped feeling that way. I knew then and there that I was not allowed to be a child; I had to be something more, regardless of whether I wanted to or not or whether I was ready for that kind of responsibility or not.

> *Once you know the truth, it may haunt you even more than all those possibilities you imagined.*

However, when my father opened up and shared personal confessions about his past life, that information was on a much deeper level. It was the moment I realized my parents had been clueless for most of their lives, maybe forever even. The decisions they made and the reasoning behind them were far worse than I had ever imagined. Just think of the fact that he made these confessions to a teen who was fast approaching when she would grow into a young adult. I was just a senior in high school, expecting to graduate a few months later and go on to college to prepare myself for adulthood.

Even his decision to come and confide in me these

personal details of his and Ursula's life was questionable, to say the least. After everything I'd been through as a child, his confessions clarified some things, and some missing pieces of the puzzle became visible. Still, that moment in time was far from ideal, as it only added to my perception of being an unwanted child. It only confirmed that I was right, and knowing that it wasn't just a feeling but the actual truth, provoked yet another trauma. It was as if I didn't have enough of those piled up at that point in my life. But hey, who's keeping track, right?

Yet again, nobody asked for my opinion; my father just stood there at my doorstep one evening. He sat down on the couch in front of me and started talking. Of course, this happened on more than one occasion, and as I gained more information, I just had to know more—even though I knew the information would not benefit me; it's like when someone tells you, "Don't look," but then you instantly look anyway. It's just human nature, I presume, and I have always been curious. In the end, it did give me the missing pieces to fill in the blanks, at least some of them. I heard only his version; we know every story has at least two sides. In the end, we all see life through our own set of glasses.

The irony is that when you don't know, your mind gets cluttered with possibilities, especially when you have a vivid imagination, as I do. But once you know the truth, it may haunt you even more than all those possibilities you imagined. For me, that has been the case ever since.

A LONELY CHILD'S REALITY

The first memory I can recall is of my father.

I'm lying in a white crib, and I'm looking at the ceiling, which is more of a gray than a white tone. There are two big doors on my left, one of which opens. I see him. He hovers over the crib and smiles at me. He said some things, too, but I only remember his face and expression. This is the first memory I have of my life, and as he confirmed to me later, that took place when I was staying in the hospital to get my tonsils removed. I must have been five years old at that time.

Why do I mention this memory? Because it confirms the sentiment that I always felt toward him, as he was the figure I looked up to. He was the person I held on to when things were rough; he was the only one who made me feel loved during my childhood. My father passed away in 2020, and when I wrote his eulogy, I referred to the childhood memories I had of him; they were some of the only positive ones I had growing up.

My father worked in hospitality; he was a self-made cook, as he hadn't studied the culinary arts. He began his career as a waiter and moved on to the kitchen toward the end. Working in restaurants meant long hours and little free time, so I missed him a lot in my younger years, as he was absent most of the time. For years, we only saw each other in the mornings when he took me to school and in the late afternoons when he got up from his nap and returned to work. That was it, except for some Wednesdays when he came home from work and went right to bed for his afternoon nap between shifts. And I also saw him on Sundays, of course, when the restaurant was closed. He had ten days off in August; that's when we could spend the most time together. We would see some family abroad, and those days always flew by.

> *I often wondered how my life would have been if I'd had more family around.*

We had no other family in Belgium, and when I watched grandparents pick up their grandchildren at school or heard kids talk about the fun time they had spent with their cousins, I felt sad. I felt sad because, even though I had a large family, I didn't have any of that. The irony is I have a huge family, but they are all abroad. In those days, there were no cell phones, WhatsApp, or email, so keeping in touch was much more complex and expensive. We would see some family during those ten days in

August but never the whole other part of the family. We heard some of them over the phone at Christmas and New Year's. Some other family members would send postcards or letters once in a while.

I often wondered how my life would have been if I had family around; maybe I wouldn't have been so lonely. Maybe Ursula wouldn't have been so hurtful to me because she would have been happier. Happy people don't want to hurt others; that's how I see it. But these are all suppositions; I'll never know for sure. There is no use wasting time, as it won't change the way it actually was.

Better luck with my godfather and godmother, right? Not so much, as my godfather was my father's youngest brother who lived abroad, too, and my godmother was one of his daughters. Since I was raised a Catholic, whenever there was an official event, I needed surrogates to take their place. Otherwise, the ceremony couldn't take place. The only time they were present was for my baptism, but of course, I have no recollection of that day, as I was only a few weeks old. I have no memories of them at all, except for the few pictures I have of those days.

Ursula started talking to an elderly couple who lived right next door to us, as our balconies were right in front of each other. Ursula found out they had no kids, which meant they didn't have any grandchildren either, so she sent me to their place. It felt so awkward for me, as they were strangers; I had a hard time opening up to anyone, let alone strangers. Yet again, nobody asked for my opinion, so I just had to go. Ursula even made me go to church with them on Sundays. Yes, you heard me; I had to go to church on Sundays as the only member of my family. Even if I never understood why, I still had to do what I was told.

I don't remember when I started going to the neighbors, but I do remember it lasted as long as we lived there (until I was almost thirteen). What would we do in our time together? They baked pancakes and mousse au chocolate. The lady was a painter, and she let me try to do some experimenting of my own. My father was a hobby painter, too, but I didn't inherit his talent. It's notorious that I have two left hands, and I am quite the clumsy gal. But I did enjoy it; I painted with oil-based paint on big canvases. I held on to those paint tubes for many years; I kept them in a drawer, thinking I might pick them up someday and try again. That day hasn't come yet, but you never know.

So, even if I never understood why Ursula would send me over to strangers, I'm glad I got to know them, and I appreciate the time they spent with me. After we moved, we lost touch, and I remember Ursula telling me about their passing some years later. I felt guilty because I did not keep in touch at all, and I felt I should have. Even if I was obliged to spend time with them as a child, their affection for me was genuine, and I could have shown more gratitude. But as I spent time with them, I was more consumed by the sensation that Ursula had shipped me away, as if I were a package she wanted to get rid of—some space-filling box she wanted to get out of her way.

I did my best to make her forget I was even there.

The apartment we lived in had two bedrooms, and I had to share my parents' bedroom. My bed was next to the wall, which was on the other side of the building's hallway. We lived on the top floor, and the elevator shaft was next to our door. That elevator freaked me out, as you could make it go up and down automatically, without anyone inside. And many times, when I was lying in bed at night, I could hear the elevator come up to our floor without anyone going in or out. I remember shivering as my imagination made up some vivid reasons why this happened. Neither of them were made for kids.

There was just enough room for their double bed, my single bed, and a big closet. My bed was just at arm's length, separated from theirs; a nightstand separated the beds. It was Ursula who slept closest to me, which made me feel quite uncomfortable, as she used to watch over me like a hawk all the time. She was ready to lash out at me for whatever reason she felt appropriate, reasons she had no problem finding.

In that apartment, I wasn't allowed to make any mess while playing, which is impossible, to say the least. If you have children, you know I'm right; the best part of being a child is to be able to make some mess and release your creativity into this world. Moreover, I wasn't allowed to make noise either—another specific feature of being a child—so playing wasn't just some free time; it took dedication and courage. Any innocent playtime could unleash a fierce reaction from her side, so it had to be worth the risk. I did my best to make her forget I was even there, but I was still a child and needed to play because that's what children do.

I loved to play "teacher" and would set up my dolls and teddy bears around the table and teach them lessons. One of the things I enjoyed most was correcting their errors on paper. That's funny because, as a writer, I enjoy rewriting the most; I have always been a control freak, so I suppose this is one of those traits. But the game I loved to play the most was solving crimes. I was inspired by television shows like Columbo, where you would see the delict first and watch the Lieutenant come up with the solution afterward. I had a little notepad and walked around questioning my students from my class. At that point, I dreamt of becoming a criminologist, but then I saw the horror movie *Silence of the Lambs* and watched Jodie Foster fulfill that role. I knew then that it wasn't for me. I was way too sensitive for that job.

> *To this day, that is still the essence of who I am.*

Another way I entertained myself was by hosting a

radio show. I had a small tape recorder, which I used to record my voice and make my commercials with my synthesizer. To start recording my show, I just had to take my tape recorder and press the two buttons on it at the same time. I still remember the tape's sound as it rolled inside the device. I found one of the tapes amid some old stuff at home a few months ago. It was like getting into the *DeLorean*, leaving today's world, and instantly finding myself back in my old room. I listened to the tape with my husband and kids. In the beginning, it was funny; I was amazed by the amount of creativity the recording represented. By copying what I heard on TV and the radio, I managed to imitate various voices, tones, and characters.

However, we all got silent when we stopped laughing at the absurdity of what I was saying and started to listen to the words I was using. Even though it was dark and sad, the talk show was quite clever. What I remembered about my radio show was it being all fun and games, but now I realize it was serious and realistic. Interviewing physicians and smokers about cancer. So I was shocked by the level of realism and adult content; I wondered why such a little child would talk about such serious and life-altering events in her worry-free time. After hearing the recording I got emotional listening to my younger self. I felt a deep sense of sympathy, solitude, and sorrow. And I wanted to reach out and hug myself, as I felt like that child needed one. It became clear that I hosted my radio show to create a parallel world of my own, to feel less alone, and to feel useful. And to this day, that is still the essence of who I am.

The problem-solving part of who I am, which I used

in all my playtime, remained intact over the years. It's a feature I still own today. I've often wondered if that was an innate trait or if I learned it because of how I grew up. I have a great sense of justice and a significant need for truth. However, I lacked both of those values at home. Moreover, I witnessed so many lies and deceit that I now have zero tolerance for the latter. Even as a child, I could never grasp why people can't tell the truth. Why can't people be honest and own up to what they do? I never understood why adults, at least those I grew up with, would prefer to lie instead of taking responsibility for their actions.

It's an absurd way of life, as the truth usually catches up quickly, and the consequences are far more significant than if you had just told the truth in the first place. Why would you do this to yourself and others?

> *My vivid imagination saved me more than once.*

My imagination was a soft way to escape from the toxic environment I lived in. I was lost and scared, and I spent most of my childhood alone. In school, I didn't relate to my classmates, as I was introverted and highly sensitive. My vivid imagination saved me more than once. I didn't spend my time only playing games; I started writing at the young age of eight. For example, I wrote a fantasy story about a young girl growing up in a random family, but one night, she was called to fulfill a greater purpose. She appeared to have special powers and needed to leave her family to battle an evil being to save the world.

Writing stories was my way of living an adventure in another world and, most of all, feeling strong beyond measure—a drastic contrast to how powerless I felt every single day. I remember having a red coat with an oversized hoodie, and when I walked alone on the playground at school, I would put the hoodie up and imagine I was a powerful creature. I had a soft spot for Japanese Anime; at the time, I was a big fan of Saint Seiya. I dreamt of being Princess Athena, lying there with the golden arrow in my chest, about to die, and then Pegasus and the others would risk their lives to save me. I needed to be saved, as I wasn't able to protect myself.

The only power I felt was within, as if something inside me kept protecting me somehow from what was happening in the outside world. I kept to myself most of the time and didn't confide in anyone. No matter where I was, but especially at home, I kept silent. I did my best to make her forget I was even there. I hoped that would decrease the chance of her lashing out at me. But when you're so little, your home is your entire world; it's much more than just a roof above your head. At the very least, it should be your safe haven, where you have people who love you and cherish you. People, you should be able to trust without a doubt. But my house was nothing other than that, a brick apartment with a roof over my head. I wasn't safe from harm. I didn't feel loved or cherished, and I definitely couldn't trust her.

I must have been an awful child.

A thing Ursula did that drove me mad was talking ill about me when I was not in the room, yet close enough for me to hear what she was saying. It hurt me so much that I felt more invisible than I thought. It was as if she didn't even acknowledge that I was a person with feelings. I remember we had a cupboard with a large mirror standing in the corridor, separating the living room from the bedrooms. I can still see myself standing there, looking at myself in the mirror and watching myself cry my heart out. But I made sure I did it quietly so Ursula couldn't hear me. I wouldn't give her the bonus of seeing that she had hurt me with her words.

I can see myself looking at my reflection in the mirror and trying to keep sane, attempting to hold it together and not break the freakin' mirror. Emotional abuse was one of her favorites when it came to hurting me, but it wasn't the only way Ursula used. Her other favorite methods included wooden cooking spoons, leather buckles, and even her bare hands. The sting of those attacks lasted for only a short time, yet her vile words are still in my mind today.

You must think I must have been a wicked child, a queen of mischief; I wish I had been naughty! At least I would have known why Ursula mistreated me that way. Growing up and understanding more about my parents' life, the only motivation (not that there is any valid motivation to mistreat a child) I could come up with was that she used me as a form of stress relief. For her, I must have been a human punching bag of some kind. She must have been so unhappy and frustrated about her life that she needed a way to relieve herself. Not being a child of love, what better target to choose? It's not as if I could defend myself or get away somehow. My father worked most of the time and was never home, and I was already asleep when he returned at night.

But that doesn't mean he wasn't aware of what was happening at home. Ursula made no effort to keep up appearances, at least not to him. Ursula did an excellent job of keeping it all from the public eye; always friendly to others and even helpful. Nobody at school ever questioned me about the dysfunctional situation I lived in because they had no clue. To say the truth, I did an excellent job at keeping it to myself as well.

There's one specific situation I remember: I was in the classroom, and we were about to make some art for Mother's Day. Before we started, the teacher asked, as a rhetorical question, who didn't love their mom. I heard the other kids laugh, but I took it seriously and raised my hand. I can still see the scene play out before me, the teacher looking at me, clueless about what was going on and how she was supposed to react to me. She didn't know what to do, so she just ignored me and continued with her lesson. Her inaction didn't surprise me, as I was used to being invisible.

She made me drink it.

Ursula used to heat some milk on the stove and give it to me to drink before I went to sleep. But I remember she must have been distracted one night, as the milk burned. I still remember the smell of it. I didn't need to taste it to know that it was better to toss it away. She should have just warmed up some new milk for me. But no, she didn't, and she made me drink it all. . . .

It might not sound like a big deal to some, but I can still smell and taste that burned cup of milk to this day. And it caused me to dislike milk from that evening on, as my body still remembers, and even if you gave me a cup of the best milk in the world, you still couldn't fool me. I would still smell and taste that cup of burned milk from when I was little. I can only cope with drinking milk if its taste is mixed with other dominant flavors.

It did impact my daily life a bit like a lactose intolerance; I need to protect myself from wherever I go. It makes you realize how some decisions, no matter how insignificant they might seem, can have a significant influence on your life.

He was often complicit in her behavior.

When I became an adult, one of my arguments with my father was my attempt to make him realize how he had been complicit in her behavior all those years. You're complicit when you know what is happening and don't do anything about it. His way of "helping" me was to take me out on Sundays when it was his day of rest from work. He would take me to the market, walk through the university campus, and have hot drinks. It became a routine, and I enjoyed our time together away from the house. Yet, it didn't solve anything.

As soon as we returned home, he would go to the basement, where he had a workshop. My father was an artist; he painted and made miniature boats, and he was very skilled with his hands. Our basement gave me the chills; Ursula would send me down to call him for dinner, and it scared me to go in that part of the house. The basement was like a maze, with different corridors and lights working with a timer and an actual ticking clock. And it happened more than once that the lights went out, and I was left in the dark when I moved too slowly.

He spent hours in that dark place, so even when he was off from work, he still wasn't present in the apartment.

Like me, he did everything he could to avoid being in the house, but other than my time in school, I didn't have many occasions to get away. I could go to the parking lot and play there, and on the weekend, I became a Girl Scout. Unfortunately, I was an introvert trying to get along with a large group of people, most of them very outgoing and sporty. It wasn't a great fit for me, but it was still better than being home.

I learned to wear a mask to fit in those situations somehow, and I would act silly like a clown and make others laugh. They thought I was weird anyway, so at least they could consider it in a fun way. Some days, I did a good job; once the first laughter started, I knew the day would be successful. But other days, I didn't make them to laugh at all, and those days, I felt like more of a failure. If I couldn't even make them laugh, what did I have to offer this world?

But I didn't have another choice, as I didn't know who I was, so this mask was my best option. Ursula told me I wasn't worth anything, nobody would care or love me, I wouldn't achieve anything in life, etc. Ursula did a good job of breaking my spirit down; and went so far as to make me forget who I was to start with. And it took me years to find myself again. With everything that was going on at home, the mask of my fake "happy self" became a suitable option for quite some time.

If even my father avoided being in the house with her, I'm sure you can imagine how this impacted our family. The toxicity began at the root, the relationship between Ursula and my father. They didn't have the foundations needed to be a loving couple, and that influenced everything else, infecting it all, as a matter of fact. Neither one of them attempted to change things to make them better. They chose to keep it going and keep up appearances for the outside world.

The little time they spent together consisted of fighting, name-calling, and accusations. My father had a passive personality, so he would let her emit all of her anger toward him and wait for it to pass. They never resolved their arguments or fixed the problems plaguing our homelife. In all those years, I never heard positive communication between them, only hostility and egoism. Let alone some regard towards a child, listening to it all, absorbing their negativity to the core.

There was no trust, affection, or respect whatsoever.

Growing up in the eighties, having separated parents was an exception, but I knew some kids with divorced parents. They didn't like it and complained about having separate houses with their stuff divided between each home. It sounded like a dream come true to me; I was envious of them, hoping I would be so lucky. I remember conversing with my father about a possible separation, and I expressed my wish to stay with him if my parents ever divorced. But that event never occurred, and he never mentioned it again.

Secrets were conventional to them, so having a truthful conversation was impossible. Perhaps my parents thought it was beneficial for their relationship, but it wasn't. I suppose it was all clear to me—more than it was to them. And they didn't think I had rights—not even the right to grow up in a peaceful, loving home, feeling safe and sound—since I was only a child.

Xenophobia

When I started school, I didn't know the local language. I remember sitting in the classroom with my back against the wall, looking around and wondering what all those strange-sounding words meant. The other kids were playing with each other; the teacher was interacting with them, and they were all smiling. What were they smiling about? I wanted to smile like that, too, but I had no reason to.

In time, I learned that the younger you are, the faster you learn a new language. You absorb the information like a sponge. Of course, my level of vocabulary and knowledge wasn't anywhere near the level of the other kids, but I managed to understand them well and express myself. However, the other kids noticed I was not like them in many ways. Besides the language, I had other habits, for instance, food, clothes, and behavior. But they picked on me the most for speaking a foreign language.

The thing is, I didn't even understand that I was foreign to begin with. I didn't think about what it meant that they spoke another language, the one I didn't know until I went to school. So, one day, when some kids yelled, "Go back to your country," at me, I was shocked and confused. What were they talking about? What did they mean by "another country?" At that age, I'm talking about kindergarten, the term "country" is quite abstract. In the end, I was born in the same place as them, and I didn't know any other place than this one.

As they kept yelling the same sentence, day after day, I just confronted Ursula while we were walking back home one day. And she said we came from Italy. Well, I still remember the feeling when the light went on in my mind that day when she told me that. It was as if a video game had unlocked a secret door, and I got to enter a whole new world, one I didn't even know existed. From that moment on, I embraced that knowledge and my Italian heritage with open arms, and I've never let go since. I'm proud of being Italian and have passed on my legacy to my kids.

Even though the words those kids kept saying hurt me, especially with their tone and the intensity of their wording, I never thought they were being racist. I soon realized those kids were mocking what they didn't understand. And they probably just learned those words from what they overheard their parents say at home. I assumed the concept of "country" must have been abstract to them too. Their mocking insults continued throughout elementary school, but I couldn't care less about it. I was proud of my provenance, and that's a powerful feeling.

Fear of abandonment

I remember sitting on a cold wooden bench in the schoolyard, waiting to be picked up after school. I watched as all the other kids got picked up by their moms with bright smiles on their faces and big, comforting hugs. They all got picked up one by one until just a few kids remained with me. I couldn't see the entrance, as a small tunnel separated the schoolyard from the main entrance. However, I could hear the parents' footsteps as they came, depending on what kind of shoes they wore. The sound was quite loud in the small tunnel's closed-in space.

Whenever I recognized a fast-paced walk, I thought it was my turn to be picked up. But I was wrong most of the time. My heart was beating heavily in my chest, and my fear of abandonment got higher every time my hope went up and down again. When you're an unwanted child, you sense that your fear could become a reality. Why would Ursula pick me up if she resented my very existence?

I figured the best way to get rid of me was to leave me at school one day. Eventually, she always came to pick me up, even if she let me wait till I was at the end of my rope. I had to relive my anxiety almost every single day of the week. Why was she late? I never found out, as she never offered any excuse or explanation. Why would she even bother to tell me, as she didn't care about how I felt?

I've had to endure a dog bite twice in my life.

That's another "amusing" thing that happened to me, or rather, that Ursula let happen to me, when I was a kid. When a dog bites, it's never their fault; it's the responsibility of the dog's owner. And if a dog bites a child, the responsibility also lies with the child's educator. In both cases, I'm referring to their parents. So, how could this happen twice?

The first time, I must have been four years old, maybe five; the dog was our pet, a Pekinese. I noticed the dog was on the terrace, and it looked like it was stuck in the garbage bin. I thought it was in trouble and couldn't get out of the bin on its own. The dog was upside down, its tail sticking out of the bin. I decided to help the dog, and as I was pulling it out, the dog turned around and bit me—right in the middle of my face. I remember going back inside, and Ursula began to scream when she saw me. Her reaction made me scared, as I didn't understand what was going on. To help me understand, she put me in front of the mirror in the hallway so I could see for myself. I had an open wound on my face, and blood was pouring onto my clothes; I began to cry and scream too. When the ambulance arrived, multiple paramedics had to hold me down on the way to the hospital. I didn't want to be touched. That experience scarred me for life.

The second time was about a year or two later, when we were on our summer vacation with our family abroad. My cousins went off to play soccer at a nearby field, and there were some tourists there with their dog—a German shepherd. I was bored, so I started to play with the dog. I thought riding on its back like a pony would be fun. The dog was so big to me. I guess the dog disagreed, so it shook its head, making me fall. As I was lying on my back, he bit me on my left forearm, but he released his bite right away. It was clear the dog didn't want to hurt me; it was just frustrated by me riding it.

I still remember the open wound, as it looked like a scene I'd seen in a sci-fi series called *V* that I watched on television. The protagonists were alien body shifters, and they looked like snakes. It all happened so fast, the tourists took their dog and split. Everyone else left the pitch. A woman stayed with me and began singing in German. That's when I started to cry. Another scar for life . . .

A tragic Valentine's card

School was a tough place for me more than once in my life. Another episode that marked me happened when I was about nine years old. We were approaching Valentine's Day, and some popular girls had the idea of making a big Valentine's card for the boys in the class. I mean,

I couldn't care less, but I wanted to participate just like anyone else. Some of them put a lot of effort into making a colorful card with all the boys' names on it. One of the girls took a red lipstick from home and asked all the girls to put it on and place their lips on the card.

We had to try it out on another piece of paper first to ensure the result would look good on the card. And so I did too. But when my turn came to go to the big card, one of the girls stopped me from participating. Ursula said I couldn't because the result would make the card ugly. That hurt me a lot because of one of the bite incidents; a chunk of my upper lip got lost, leaving me a scar from the nose down. Therefore, my lips don't match; my upper lip is smaller and thinner compared to the lower one—hence the odd look when I tried the lipstick out on paper.

Inclusion wasn't a big deal back then, and I never wanted to put a lipstick kiss on any card again. They say kids can be cruel, but I think kids do as they are taught.

> *Comparison is the thief of self-esteem.*

My mom was pretty fond of one of my classmates, probably because her mom was French and, therefore, one of the few people Ursula could communicate with. However, economic and social status also played an important role. It doesn't matter what her reasoning was; she considered this girl her "ideal" for a daughter. My mom kept adding to my already complicated situation, comparing me every single day for years with this girl I used to be friends with. But her attitude toward her made me resent that girl so much that I couldn't stand her anymore. The only reason I kept inviting her to our home, or she kept inviting me to hers, was our moms.

Being compared with someone else had a significant impact on my mental health; it was the thief of the little self-esteem I had at that time. Whenever I heard her initiate a critique, beginning with the words, "Look at her," I wanted to scream in frustration. But I didn't dare to, out of fear of her retribution. I kept silent and let her rant about that girl while I was rubbing my hands or gritting my teeth to keep quiet.

But it hurt, and it damaged me for a long time. I promised myself right then and there that I would never compare my children with anyone. Children should be free to explore, express themselves, and let their personalities and character develop without judgment.

Her jealousy was unhinged.

My father was an entertainer. He loved to make people laugh, and he always had something silly to say to make you feel at ease. That's a positive feature to have when you work in hospitality, and it was great for him, especially when he worked in Italian restaurants. Since he didn't have any particular training, he started as a waiter, became a maître d'hôtel, and, in the end, went into the kitchen to become a chef.

But that feature becomes a potential threat if you are in a toxic relationship that isn't based on mutual trust or respect. And it did become a treat to her, as Ursula would always accuse him of cheating with his co-workers, to whom she would refer as whores. Was she right? She might've been, but that didn't give her the right to involve her innocent child in her unhinged behavior.

Ursula made no effort to hide her paranoia, and I have witnessed far too many one-way fights in which she blamed him with her colorful accusations, regardless of my being there to watch and hear. He was an Aquarius, a pacifist at heart, and did his best to avoid conflict. But when he had to face such violent behavior, he would lose his temper too.

I remember, one day, she took my hand and dragged me along for a few miles. She was ranting the entire time, again careless of me hearing what she said about my father. In fact, I believe she wanted me to listen to it, maybe to make me change my opinion of him and love him less. And then, after we had walked a ways, we arrived at the restaurant where he was working. I recognized our car parked outside. She just left me there near the car, and while she went inside, I was close enough to hear her screaming and the sound of rumble.

A few minutes later, she came out but didn't stop at our car where I stood. She went to the other end of the car and picked up something from the floor. As she came back, I could see she was holding a brick or a rock, and before I realized what was happening, I saw her throw it right through our car's windshield. I was in shock. I don't even remember saying anything or even making a sound. I was completely startled by what she did. After that, she grabbed my arm and forced me to follow her again. I don't even remember if my father came out to see what she had done; I hoped he would come and get me away from her, as her behavior frightened me. She looked and sounded like a lunatic, and I didn't want to follow her or listen to her angry statements anymore. Who knew what she might do next? But I had no choice; she had such a firm grip. I couldn't get loose from her grip on my arm.

My father went missing.

Not long after that disturbing incident, my father went missing. He just didn't come home from work, and we didn't know where he was. She was hysterical, crying desperately and talking ill about him the entire time. I didn't understand what could have happened to him, and I was so worried, but my main concern was her behavior, which was even more hurtful than her "normal day" behavior. At one point, she began accusing me, telling me he left because of me and that his absence was all my fault. It made me angry, but I knew in my heart that it couldn't be true. He was the only one who made me feel loved at times; I knew he cared for me and wouldn't leave because of me. If nothing terrible had happened to him, I knew the reason he left was because of her and him not being able to take it anymore. And even if I could understand, as I would want to do the same, I couldn't grasp why he would leave me behind with her.

When school started that September, he still hadn't returned home; I was now in the fifth grade. And I had no choice but to put my mask on at school, and I didn't mention it to anyone. I tried my best to adapt to this new situation; what choice did I have in the end? I did what I could to survive, letting her spit out her venom and waiting for her anger to fade. Then, one night, I woke up and saw her standing in the corridor right next to the entrance door, looking as if she'd seen a ghost. I wasn't in a waking state; it felt like a dream, but I remember thinking, *Oh, Dad is home*, and going back to sleep. As I woke up the following day, it appeared to be true; he was lying in their bed, and I went over and hugged him. I felt happy for that brief moment; she even looked pleased for a while.

For a couple of days, there was no word about his absence; life just resumed as if nothing had ever happened. It felt so weird and unreal, fake even, how they acted in those days. But it didn't last for long. I remember that one morning, while he was starting the car to bring me to school, I asked him what had happened and where he had gone. He didn't answer, never did, not even later on, but he told me he came back only because of me. You would assume that his answer would make me happy, but it didn't. On the contrary, I felt a huge responsibility, as if I were the sole reason for his unhappiness. I couldn't bear such a sad thought; he had his chance to leave and have a better life, but he gave it up because of me.

I was the ball and chain to him, and I didn't need that level of responsibility. I was never treated like an actual little child; there was never any regard for my innocence and my right to have a worry-free existence. I had to grow up so fast and become independent and responsible for myself. I wasn't ready to take on the responsibility for my father's life too. But nobody ever asked for my opinion.

> *I was clueless about what was happening.*

About a year later, I received an unexpected visitor in my last year in elementary school. While I was in class, the counselor came to take me out of the classroom. The counselor didn't explain a thing and just asked me to follow her to her office. When I arrived there, I saw an unknown man sitting at the table. I looked at her, asking who the stranger was, but I don't remember if I even received an answer. She just asked me to sit down in front of him. She stayed in the room, but I couldn't see her from my end.

The man took a notepad and started asking me strange questions about me and my relationship with my father. I remember still having my fake mask on, and the situation made me so nervous that I kept making jokes. But I noticed he took everything seriously and just wrote down everything I said. At that point, I understood this wasn't a time for jokes or fake masks. This appeared to be a serious matter, and I needed to focus on what he was asking, even though I still had no clue what was happening or why was he asking me these questions.

I don't remember how long it lasted. However I suppose it was like the usual lesson in class. But I remember going to the hospital to speak with a psychologist, and they asked me the same kind of weird questions. Once I got home, I could sense the tension in the air; something was definitely going on. But my parents didn't offer any explanations about what happened at school and what was happening at home. Were these events related to each other? I'm sure it was, but as always, open communication was not their method of choice. Keeping things a secret had always been their chosen way.

Shortly after, they announced we were about to move out of the apartment where I had lived all my life to move to a rental house a few miles outside the city. They offered no explanations, but I was still excited, as I would have a room of my own for the first time! Finally, I would have an inch of privacy, a door to close and separate myself from the rest of the house—a place of my own where I could feel safe and have some say about my surroundings. I could choose the color of the paint, how the furniture would be arranged in the room, and hang some posters of things I liked on the walls. The possibilities were endless, and my imagination ran loose thinking about all I could do. What a feeling of freedom! I had never felt that way before. A silver lining was drawing itself before me.

I found a passion.

In the summer of '94, I finally had more space and more opportunities to leave the house and do as kids do. Our neighborhood had a basketball court where some neighboring girls and boys gathered to play. Nothing fancy, no rules, no refs—just us kids playing around. We all brought our basketballs; I remember mine had a defect, as it had an air bell on its side. So, if I were unlucky to drop the ball on that side, it would bump away toward the other side. I guarantee it happened more than statistically possible. As a result, I had to run after my ball all the time, and I became a laughingstock to the other kids. Of course, they all had new basketballs from famous brands, each one cooler than the other, but I was happy to be able to join. It was such a breath of fresh air for me.

That summer, I spent all my afternoons (until evening hit) on the court, and the cherry on top was the ice cream truck that stopped by every night. Even if I didn't have pocket money to spend every day, I would say I wasn't hungry compared to the other kids who bought it every night. But I just enjoyed the vibe; it was just a bunch of kids playing together, enjoying their summer. Some of them I knew from school, but others I hadn't seen before.

It was a free court, open to the public, so anyone could come and play, and that was the beauty of it. It was a good trial for me to open up more, get to know other kids, have some fun, and forget the fake mask I had been wearing at school.

There was this one boy, though, that I couldn't stand. Romero wasn't part of any group from our school or the surrounding blocks. He came from another neighborhood and was one or two years older than the rest of us. I believed he was so annoying, always serious, and had a temper. You could say he really got on my nerves. I remember throwing a scoop of ice cream at him one night because I'd had enough of his arrogance. All the kids were laughing, me included, but Romero didn't have any sense of self-irony.

I was quite the tomboy.

At that age, I was quite the tomboy, wearing oversized T-shirts and wide pants. I was more comfortable hanging out with boys than girls most of the time. I had enough drama in my life and needed to have fun and be worry-free. You would think I was trying my best not to be a girl and be more like a boy. Well, if you look at my passions at that time, watching *Rocky* movies (which I still love), looking up to Bruce Lee (which I still do), playing with Legos (I'm a nerd, I know), and being a fan of soccer (yes, I still am). I guess it was the way I found to empower myself as a girl, to be more confident and less vulnerable.

But that wasn't the only reason; I had never been materialistic or superficial. Yet I had to grow up so fast and take on responsibilities, making me more serious and stressed than other kids. I didn't care about dressing a certain way, doing my hair, putting on makeup, or being popular or likable. I was used to being invisible, so I couldn't care less about what others thought about me.

I knew I wasn't worth much—at least, that's what I had been told, and I believed it. So, why even try? I just wanted to enjoy my life for once, and I didn't care about the rest. Just leave me be and let me live, period. That's what made me happy at that time. Thanks to my vivid imagination, I was able to entertain myself, at least mentally.

It was him, the boy I couldn't stand.

Once school started in September and the weather changed, our basketball season was over until the following summer. I didn't see most of those kids from that moment on. One day, when we were in the city's swimming arena for our physical education lesson and were about to leave the pool, I noticed someone I knew from the basketball court. It was Romero, the guy I couldn't stand. I told my girlfriends to look over at the showers, as that was the annoying guy I had told them about. They said he was really cute; maybe, I don't know. I never looked at him that way, so I urged myself to leave the pool before he would notice me, too, but I failed. Our eyes met right before I reached the exit, and I ignored him altogether. I remember my friends laughing with me, as they, unlike me, didn't make any effort to avoid his attention.

Then, the week after that, I felt nervous as we went to our weekly swimming lesson, as I knew Romero would likely be back for his lesson as well. My friends planted a seed in my mind, and now I couldn't act as if I didn't notice that he was cute, either. But this was all new to me; I'd had crushes before, even from a young age, but this was my first one as a teenager, when I was just about to hit puberty.

It changed how I perceived things quite a bit; I didn't want him to notice and maybe make fun of me or something. I was completely outside my comfort zone, being in my bathing suit and not in the oversized clothes he'd always seen me in before. There are no masks to wear when you are that exposed, so I just hoped Romero wouldn't show; or did I? It was all so confusing. But he did show up, just like the week before. And again, I had to walk past him to go to the pool's exit. However, this time, we had more prolonged eye contact than before. I did my best to act cool and uninterested, but I'm sure he could see my feelings clearly, as my face has always been an open book.

If you wanted to reach someone in those days, you just looked up their family name in the white pages. It was a big book that contained all the landlines of civilians within a specific area, and all those living in that area would receive a free copy each year. Having a copy of the phone book made reaching out to someone much easier, but I never expected to receive a phone call at home from him.

I mean, why would he make the effort to look me up and call me? To say what? All we ever did was argue, and we never spoke to each other at the swimming pool. But he did, and one evening, when I returned home after piano lessons, I found out Romero had called and left a message. I didn't know what to say or what to think; I was shocked. My mind went overboard thinking about all the possibilities. It was so awkward; I acted like he was a fellow student from school. Why would a boy be calling me otherwise?

This was new to me.

Later that evening, Romero called back, and I talked to him on the phone. But most of the time, I let him speak and just replied with short answers. Imagine standing in the middle of the living room, talking to a boy with your parents present. I didn't want to show how awkward and confused I was, but I was also excited, as this was a first for me. It was one of those events you remember forever. He asked if we could meet up because he wanted to talk to me; he wasn't putting his cards on the table. In those days,

I didn't have a lot of liberty; those summer nights playing basketball were gone, and as it was fall, it would get dark rather soon after school. I had a strict curfew, so hanging out after school wasn't an option either. The only option I could think of was for him to walk to our new house with me. We would be moving soon, and my parents would spend much of their free time painting at the house.

But on weekends, I was expected to go to them by myself. Since he lived near me, I asked him to walk with me, and he agreed.

That Saturday, I met him near his house, and then we headed to my new house, a few miles away. I remember very little of what we spoke about, but I remember the laid-back vibe and sharing some everyday stuff like what movie we liked. We were getting to know each other better, as if we were on a date, which we weren't. Were we? No, not really, at least not intentionally, as we walked in public without any privacy or intimacy.

As we approached my family's house, my father stopped beside the sidewalk and noticed me. I had to go with him and leave the boy behind so my dad wouldn't know we were walking together. Nobody knew about our walk or about us getting to know each other. My parents were very strict, and I didn't have any confidential mother-daughter relationship, allowing me to open up and share things about my personal life. Since I lived in that type of environment, I just kept everything to myself as usual.

My first kiss

The moment every one of us waits for when we're young, the moment we fantasize about was about to happen. I would be getting my first kiss. Romero invited me over to the underground parking garage of his apartment building. It was not much of a romantic setting, but it was far from indiscreet eyes, and that was quite important, as we didn't want to be seen by our parents.

I don't really remember what we talked about the few minutes before we kissed; I just remember the kiss itself. He went for it right away; my first kiss was a passionate one. It was a French kiss with all the works. I remember thinking this was not how I expected it to be. At the time, the television show *Baywatch* was popular, and I just watched an episode with a romantic candlelight dinner scene followed by some intimacy. I remember thinking how that seemed so amazing as I waited for my moment. But now that I was right in the middle of it, it seemed something else. It felt wet and chaotic, and I had trouble keeping up with him. I kept thinking, *Hold on; slow down.*

Yet, I was pretty pleased with myself, as I realized I could have done much worse for a first kiss. Romero was cute, one or two years older than me, and I was attracted to him. The setting could have been better; he could have made an effort to create a certain mood and make me feel I mattered to him. But overall, it wasn't that bad. It wasn't love, but he was my first kiss and the first boy who showed an interest in me. Our relationship boosted my confidence as a girl and got me hoping for true romance in my life. I longed for the opportunity to love and be loved in return, as I had so much love to give. I could feel it burning inside me, a passion waiting to collide with someone else's. Let the magic operate and live happily ever after. I was still naïve; my idea of romance was scenes from *Sissi: The Young Empress* (not the Netflix series), and I had so much to learn about what real love was all about.

A CLUELESS TEEN'S FIGHT

I started to keep a journal.

We moved right before my thirteenth birthday; it was a good opportunity for everyone, as it was long overdue. The apartment was too small for us, amplifying her frustration. This house would be a new beginning and, hopefully, a reset of our family dynamics. I was still wishing for a miracle, a magical change of mindset, making everyone happier and, therefore, kinder. Even plain tolerance, "live and let live," would have been great.

Instead, we all grew further apart, as we had separate bedrooms and more doors to separate us; the time spent together was little to none. You would think I would be happier this way, but I wasn't. Like every child I just longed for an average family with enjoyable family moments, freedom of speech, caring for each other, and showing interest in each other's lives. Just wanting a caring family and to not feel so alone anymore.

I started to keep a journal in which I would confide my day-to-day life. How many times did I begin writing, confiding in my dear friend, my journal? My habit was to write in bed right before I would put out the light on my nightstand. Sometimes, I would just share what I did that day; other times, my writing was far more intense—most of the time. I named my journal "JASPER." The name was an acronym, but I can't remember what it stood for. I recall the J stood for "jongens," which means boys in Dutch. I had many journals in my adolescence and continued in different notebooks. My first diary had a beautiful cover and a lock on the outside. The following ones became more and more random: school notebooks. They didn't even look like diaries anymore.

My habit of writing in my journal and finding a friend and some solace helped me through so much. Sharing is the first step in the healing process; otherwise, negative emotions could build up inside and consume us from within. The way one feels about sharing is up to that person, but I recommend finding a way that suits you.

First encounter with alcohol

It was February '95, the day before our class's skiing trip. One of my friends from school, who lived in the suburbs, came to spend the night at my house, as we needed to be at school at 5 a.m. That day, we spent the afternoon together visiting some school friends who lived nearby; it was nothing special, just a quick visit. When we arrived, our friends were home alone, and they had some naughty plans we had not anticipated. I was still in the clown phase, wearing my silly mask around my friends, so I hardly said no to any challenge. But I wasn't prepared at all when one of them opened the cupboard and took out the liquor bottles inside.

We wondered what they would taste like, as none of us had ever tasted them. The obvious guinea pig was . . . me . . . I didn't want to do it, and I tried to find excuses why I shouldn't, but they kept insisting until I caved. They took tall glasses, filled them each with one of the liquors, and challenged me to drink them all. I didn't know back then how bad it is to mix different kinds of drinks; I learned my lesson, to say the least. Foolishly, I drank the three different liquors, one after the other, without pausing. The next thing I remember was hearing them laugh, and I got sleepy. I couldn't see straight anymore, and I had a hard time keeping my focus.

They must have taken me to bed, as I remember lying down and looking at pictures of people I didn't know on a nightstand. Even though it felt like the room was spinning, I tried to focus properly on what I was looking at, but it didn't work. Yet, I did remember I needed to head back home, as I had a strict curfew and had no recollection of time. So, I headed downstairs and grabbed my friend, who was staying the night, urging her to leave immediately. The issue, besides the fact that I was drunk, was that we had used my bike to get to the party.

My vision was still a bit blurry, which made cycling quite challenging. It was a Saturday afternoon, so there was a lot of traffic on the roads as people went shopping. To make the journey home, I told my friend I would keep my eyes closed to focus on my movement while she told me which way to go. I realize this sounds ludicrous, but that's how it went. And it worked, amazingly; we arrived at my house in one piece and managed to get upstairs to my room without my parents seeing me.

As soon as I lay down on my bed, I felt dizzy and sick to my stomach. I vomited a few times on the floor and felt like dying. I remember seeing the peas I'd eaten for lunch floating amidst the mixed liquor. What a horrid night, and to think I had to spend the next day on a bus driving for hours to go skiing. I had to clean it all up before leaving without my parents noticing. In this case, I was fortunate for once.

It was a grave precedent, as I didn't enjoy the feeling of being under the influence one bit. And consequently, I would be careful when drinking alcohol when I get older. I would drink it as long as I enjoyed the taste and the feel; however, as soon as I felt my focus was shifting, I would stop. The legal age for drinking alcohol is only sixteen, and many referred to me as being dull or "no fun" to go out with. But I didn't care; that kind of absurd peer pressure often had the opposite effect on me, as I became even more rigid in my decision not to drink a lot.

This first encounter was an excellent lesson for me not to play with alcohol, as it messes with your head and your body. I had enough drama in my life already; I didn't need to add to it.

She didn't have my back.

As the end of the school year approached and the report card came in, I failed in math, as I expected. I had just completed my second year of secondary school and had reached my limit with that subject. Math had always been a pain in the ass. Up to that point, I . But I didn't succeed that year, at least not in that area. So, I expected summer school, another examination, or an extra engagement with additional exercises. But nothing could have prepared me for what happened instead.

So, the day came to meet with my teacher and hear her verdict, and she was quite upset with my results. She told me I could do much better than this and needed to work harder. Ursula sat beside me and agreed with my teacher the whole time through her explanation, which I also expected. However, what came next was a total shocker. Instead of proposing additional exercises throughout the summer, she advised me to repeat my entire year.

I couldn't believe this; it was an unfair situation. I wasn't a bad student; but I lacked the proper support in math and couldn't do enough to pass the course as I had in previous years. And I knew I could do better if I got extra help, but no. The teacher did not offer any additional help, as they believed I needed a wake-up call, which meant doing the school year over again. As I turned to Ursula, outraged, looking for her to back me up . . . nothing . . .

She just kept nodding and agreed with what the teacher was saying. I never got the chance to speak up, argue my side of the story, or plea in my favor, since no one else was going to. This was it; the case was closed. I had to repeat my second year of secondary school.

I remember going straight out to the backyard, standing there, wanting to scream all of my frustration and feelings of injustice out of my overloaded mind. I couldn't believe she just went along without even pleading for me. Did she think about all the efforts I had been making to do it all on my own at school? Did she mention to my teacher I wasn't getting any support whatsoever at home, not with my schoolwork or even for my emotional life? No, she did not. I don't think she ever gave me credit for it. Since the day I was born, she had always considered me a failure. This was just the universe telling her she'd been right about me all along.

Ursula didn't care about what repercussions this would have on me, on my adolescent life. This would mean I would lose all certainties, as my childhood friends would move on to the next grade, and I would be literally left behind. The third year went on to another part of the school, with a separate schoolyard and cafeteria, so I wouldn't even be apt to hang out with them at recess or during lunch. This would be a radical change for me; the little balance I had in my life, the little social life I had built, was about to disappear. And I would need to adapt again to an entirely new situation with new people.

Age fifteen: total annihilation

The perfect storm

A particular event led to the day when my life changed for the worse. It was wintertime, and I just turned fifteen a few weeks prior. After repeating my second year, over the following months, I had lost sight of my childhood friends with whom I shared the class for almost a decade. I was coping and making new friends, but it was all a balancing act, especially regarding trust and opening up. So, when a severe event occurred in my family, which didn't relate to me personally but affected my father, I felt lost and confused. But I still didn't have anyone to share my thoughts with. Once again, the adults surrounding me didn't protect me as a child; they just dumped their struggles on me to free themselves and left me alone to process them.

When we got snow that winter, I left my bike in the garage for a few days and took the bus instead. The neighborhood I moved to didn't have a good reputation, so I shied away from getting to know any of the other teens living there. The introvert in me had no reason to, and I liked to stick with what I knew and trusted, so why even try? But I wasn't feeling like myself amid this perfect storm. I felt mentally adrift, attempting to find my way through the rough sea, doing my best to stay afloat. For me, taking the bus meant sharing it with some of the other teens from the neighborhood. They were interested in me; they had lived there longer and knew I was the new teen on the block. I had never given them the time of day before, but now I was stuck with them on the bus. There was nowhere to go and nowhere to hide. I felt invisible for most of my life, so I figured they had no reason to want to get to know me.

The thing about predators is they can sense when their prey is up for grabs, and they adapt their behavior to approach it without scaring it away. The thing is, I wasn't aware of them being predators, let alone me being prey. I remember, one day, they just started talking to me, asking me everyday things about school. And I must say I enjoyed the attention, moreover the fact of being seen and them caring about how I felt. I should have known their attention was too good to be true; why would complete strangers find me interesting enough to want to get to know me further and even care about me? That's just weird, right? But the lost sailor I was at that moment needed their attention so much. I did my best at school to keep it all in; the matters in my head were just so heavy a load, but I was on a ship with no port to go to. So, I took the olive branch I believed those teens were giving me, and I didn't stop to reflect on what I was getting into.

When one of them offered a shoulder to cry on, an ear to talk to; it sounded like heaven. The following Monday morning, he invited me over to his place, right around the corner from where I lived. It was so out of character for me, not only to accept such an invitation from someone

I hardly knew but also to skip school. I was a ship lost in the rough sea and needed to unload my cargo as soon as possible—so I agreed to do it with him.

Body-jacked

I took my bike and rode to his house. To my surprise, there was a friend of his in the living room as I came in. Damien was part of the "bus crew" as well. Soon after my arrival, he invited me upstairs; I followed without questioning, as I supposed he wanted to talk to me in private. We entered the room; I entered first and walked towards the window overlooking the street. At that point, I heard the door close behind me, locking even. So, I turned to look at it and caught him still standing there with his hand on the key.

At that moment, I didn't understand what was happening right away. It felt odd, but I couldn't grasp the seriousness of this event. Damien gave me a choice: to collaborate or to be forced. I remember the feeling of being frozen right in the spot where I was standing; just for a second, I looked back at the window, contemplating the possibility of throwing myself out the window. But then again, I needed to be in control to get my body to do that, but I wasn't in control anymore. I was completely frozen, lost in confusion, as my mind went blank. I wasn't thinking straight; it was so strange for me to have such an incapacitated brain, yet at that moment, everything was a blur.

I describe what happened to me by using the term "body-jacked." Afterward, it felt as if Damien had taken hold of me, somehow stopped my brain from functioning, and ran away with my body. It was as if I stood there as I watched him having his way with my body; witnessing it all, but I couldn't do anything about it. So, I stood there nearby, but I wasn't in there anymore. Damien got total control.

After he was done with my body, he abandoned it on the spot. My conscience returned to its station and went into autopilot mode. Then I got dressed while he stood there, acting as if nothing particular had happened, as so many others had before that day. But I just wanted to leave, so I acted as normal as possible, ensuring Damien would just let me go. And he did.

Innocence lost

When I skipped school that morning, I planned to still go to school as soon as possible so I wouldn't miss an entire day. But my feet took me straight home. I couldn't even think of a plausible reason to give her for being home so early on a school day, and I just wanted to feel safe again. Little did I know that I would never feel safe another day in my life. Aside from what I endured as a child, I now had another traumatic experience to cope with, and I grew more anxious from that moment on. But I was unaware of the consequences; I wasn't thinking of anything other than getting home and being able to close a door between me and the outside world. Before, I was terrified of being at home, but now I had learned that danger was also on the other side of the front door.

That boy took my innocence, something pure and irreplaceable, something I never even knew I had. Yet, it turned out to be invaluable, and I would never get it back again. That boy took a part of me and left me broken beyond repair. But I didn't have the tools to realize the life-altering consequences that incident would have in my life. I was still shocked, oblivious to what had happened and what it meant.

As I sat at my piano and looked at my reflection in the satin-like sheen, I remember thinking: *Who are you?* I didn't know who I was looking at; the reflection looked the same as it had on other days, but my eyes weren't. Something within shifted, and it showed in my eyes, even when my face masked it to the outside world. My eyes didn't lie; they never could. And I just sat there for a while, my hands on the keys, but no movement came from them, so there was no sound either; I kept both hands on the piano, but they stood still.

And I did my best to hide that shift from anyone else; that wasn't such an arduous task, as I was pretty invisible anyway. I would just put my mask back on and keep going as I had before. Maybe I could forget in time? Or could I play some mental trick to make me believe what happened wasn't a big deal, after all? Yeah, right; who was I kidding?

When my parents found out

It wasn't long before my parents found out about what had happened, at least their version, which had nothing to do with the truth. But then again, when did they ever show an interest in the truth and what's real? I sat in my piano seat while they stood there looking at me, shocked and disappointed. I felt somewhat calm, as that situation was so unusual for me. Before then, they had showed very little interest in my life or what I was going through. I almost felt relieved, as I thought I could finally unload my heavy excess baggage at a safe port. But that wasn't the case at all; how stupid of me . . .

They didn't ask me anything; they just yelled at me, and I will never forget how my father called me a whore before storming out of the room. Our relationship was never the same after that, as it hurt me at such a personal level, and I still can't comprehend how he could have been so cruel. I would expect it from her but not from my father, who I looked up to as a child and was my only source of affection and some happy moments growing up. But that day, those special moments were all just a distant memory. He judged me in the worst way and added a fresh scar to my already stigmatized body.

I was in a frantic state.

I still remember that night. I was extremely hurt, and I was crying and screaming in my room.
And in that frantic state, I wrote giant letters all over the pages in my journal; my teardrops made them wet, smearing the ink as I wrote.

In my journal, I unloaded all of my anger, frustration, and hatred.

When I finally came by, I took some tape and emptied the entire roll over my journal, making sure nobody, including me, would ever read it. And it felt like I was putting all those negative feelings into Pandora's box, locking them up to be lost forever.

That journal remained in my nightstand for as long as I can remember. I knew it was there, but I never looked back or touched it. It's safe to say my habit of keeping a journal, finding a friend and some solace in my writing, helped me through so much. Sharing is the first step in healing; otherwise, those negative feelings can build up inside and consume you from within.

Destruction of self

My father called me a whore, and her silent agreement destroyed me even more than I ever thought possible. How could the ones who put me on this earth not know me at all? How could the people who should know me best, even for a moment, believe I was anything like the names they called me? I was called so many bad names growing up, but this one was the worst by far. Yes, I had some crushes and relationships, but it never went further than French kissing. I never allowed anyone to touch my body, not even myself. Even if I had just turned fifteen, but I was still a child in so many ways, innocent and not sexually active at all. What they called me could not have been further from the truth of who I really was.

Before that day, I had never felt so lost and alone, and I felt dirty and disposable. And if my parents thought I was a whore, maybe they were right. So, I began to act like the new definition of myself and started destroying whatever innocence I had left. I hated myself so much and felt no one could ever love me, so why bother trying to be a good person? I had no virtue to protect, integrity to preserve, or immaculate body to safeguard.

The truth is, I didn't give a shit anymore.

What followed was pure darkness, a numb state of mind, and a complete loss of self-esteem. I was invisible to my family, people at school, and even myself. But I wasn't able to do anything else at that time; having no guidance, no support, and no self-care made me reach rock bottom in the months that followed. But not completely.

A sense of awareness awakened from its senseless state when I was about to hit that bottom. I'm talking about taking drugs, which would have been the next step if I didn't stop in time. There still was some sense of reason within me, and I stopped myself before I could do some irrevocable damage to my body and mind.

Why did I choose not to take drugs? I already had little to no control over my life whatsoever; others had already decided so much for me, so why would I risk losing the little control I still had? You don't know what effect drugs will have on you, physically or mentally; would you be able to stop after trying, or would you become addicted to it? No, I didn't want to give up complete control over my life, and I didn't want to jeopardize my future and the possibilities that lay ahead. I might have lost my innocence, but I didn't lose my strong will to live. And I owed it to myself, after going through so much darkness already, to at least give it my best shot to try and make it better—to make it count.

For the first time in months, I walked up to my father and asked him to send me away that summer, no questions asked. I must have been very convincing, as he took me seriously and reached out to my family in southern Italy. It was all arranged in a matter of days; I would stay with my family (who I had never met or spoken to) for the entire summer. I'm so grateful to myself for waking up in time and to my father for answering the call when I asked for help. Going away to Italy that summer saved my life. I genuinely don't know what would have happened to me if I hadn't. My strong will to live had won and taken me out of the darkness I was stuck in.

Italian renaissance

I was so eager to leave; even though I'm an introvert by nature, I was about to take a plane for the first time and go to an unknown city by myself—to stay with people I had never met before. Crazy, right? But I couldn't wait to get there and start over. I felt in my soul this was what I needed to do to save myself from further harm. I punished myself enough for the past months, thinking I deserved to be, but it had to stop before reaching a point of no return. Therefore, I was determined to not give up on life.

When I landed and found my way out of the baggage claim area, I was relieved to see a familiar face amongst the crowd. One of my cousins, whom I knew from previous vacations, also visited our family, so she came when she heard I was flying in. It was a good idea, as it felt less awkward to us all.

But the ice melted soon; they were very welcoming

and opened their home to me without hesitation. It felt so unreal that people I had never seen were happy about getting to know me. I grew up without family in our country, so being able to visit with dozens of cousins, aunts, and uncles was an out-of-this-world experience.

I felt lucky to be there with my aunt, uncle, and their four kids. My aunt was so open and kind and caring. I watched as she taught her daughters how to cook, and she asked me to join them. She asked me to tell her about myself, about my hopes and dreams. It was odd having someone interested in me, wanting to know how I felt. They had some fights, too, but they didn't last. They communicated with each other and sorted things out. After a fight, they would make up, hug it out, and continue their lives on a positive note.

I remember thinking about how my life would have been growing up over there with my family; maybe it would all have been different—or at least less horrible. Could I have compensated for the lack of love and affection at home with this kind of attention? Who knows if I would have been less frightened and more open.

That time with my family gave me hope for a better future; it reassured me that I wasn't dead inside and was still capable of love. I craved it so much, and my summer in Italy made me realize how much I needed it. I felt so good and proud being there, belonging to such a wonderful place, and I dreamt about moving there after I graduated. My love for Italy had already been a big part of my life, but after that summer, it became everlasting, something no one could ever take away from me, and that made me feel rich. When you belong, you feel less alone, like you're proudly part of something greater than yourself. Those feelings filled part of the void in my chest, made me feel more alive than ever before. And empowered me to have faith.

A damaged girl's spring: coming-of-age

My summer in Italy was a turning point.

Meeting my family and getting a real sense of belonging boosted my self-confidence. It gave me a new belief that my life was far from over; who knows how many new adventures I will have in the future? I came to life in Italy and knew I would return as many times as possible to reload and revive that amazing feeling I experienced that summer. Even if I understood I wouldn't be able to forget the past year, but I would do my best to ascent to a new life despite it. I still had so much to discover, so much to learn, and so much to look forward to. And I wouldn't let my trauma hold me back; Instead, I would do all I could to make the most of it.

The school year was off to a great start; many new faces joined my class, and many others left. It felt like a chance to start over. There was no prejudice from previous classmates, as they weren't there; what a relief. I was so lucky to hit it off right away with one of the new girls; she became my best friend that year. Even if the beginning was awkward, as we were sharing personal things, we had a special connection; it appeared her grandmother had been our landlord in the past. Talk about living on different economic levels. But it didn't matter to her or me; we accepted each other for who we were, not for our parents' status. That school year was the best one I ever had, filled with genuine friendships, fun, and (the cherry on top) love.

One regret

After all that I had been through growing up, I had zero tolerance for lies and deceit. Therefore, I promised myself that I would draw a red line that no one could never cross and that I would choose the people in my life carefully. Past events made me become so mistrusting and needed the tools to protect myself from harm, as I had been through so much already. I didn't yet have the maturity for nuance and to judge events based on their specific features, not to judge upfront without a proper, thoughtful process. I was categorical at that time; it was my way of coping and prioritizing, as I didn't know any other way.

I was happy and hopeful when I fell in love with one of my classmates during a trip to Paris. Edward wasn't a stranger; we had been sharing our school life for months. We just had never had the opportunity to talk and get to know each other better prior to that school trip. The situation brought us together, as it got us talking, and we found out we shared some things in common. I'd never thought about him in a romantic way before, and I'm sure he didn't think about me that way either. However, while we were on the bus taking us back home, I realized I kept reminiscing about our trip and thinking about him with a smile. And I didn't want it to end; I wanted it to continue and maybe grow into something more.

A contradictory aspect of my character is that despite being an introvert when it comes to love, I was the hunter. And when I was attracted to someone, I didn't hesitate to make the first move and ask them out. And so, as soon as our bus arrived at our school, I asked him out and Edward accepted. What would follow was a sincere teenage romance. He confirmed that he had the same feelings about me, and our connection felt promising. It was a first for both of us; it was my first positive relationship, and it felt so natural. There was no drama, which felt so unreal.

In retrospect, maybe that was one of the reasons I sabotaged it unconsciously. My anxieties took over at the first reddish flag and left me harmless. This is the one regret I have about how I ended things with him. Edward didn't deserve it, nor did I, but I was clueless about what love was at that time. I thought I was doing the right thing, holding on to my strict values and letting my head decide, despite my feelings for him.

Yes, he lied to me about a promise he didn't keep, but

the reason I knew he lied was that he told me himself. But I was so disappointed, like a myth falling off his pedestal, that I couldn't see that the fact Edward told me the truth and apologized mattered more than his lie. No, I could only see that he lied, period. My zero tolerance didn't leave any room for interpretation. I know now how rare it is for people to tell the truth, take responsibility for their actions, and apologize for it. But I didn't back then, and I placed so much trust in him that I couldn't see beyond his one mistake. And that's the one regret I'll always have.

Writing this memoir, I dreamt about him and looked him up online. I wanted to make sure Edward was alright, leading a happy life, and maybe feel a little less guilty about how I acted when I was sixteen. But I found out he passed away; I don't know how long ago or what caused his early passing, but the weird part was it felt as if I already knew it somehow. To read the news of his passing on his social media made me sad, but it didn't come as a surprise. That's so inexplicable, as we haven't seen each other and haven't spoken in almost thirty years. I have no mutual friends or other sources, but I still feel I knew he was gone. The only relief is that wherever he is now, Edward knows I regret ending our relationship the way I did and not realizing what a good guy he was. He was far better than the ones who followed until I met my husband more than a decade later. I cherish the sweet moments we shared and am thankful for having known and loved him.

In memoriam.

Elements of nature

I couldn't imagine I would meet another guy just a few weeks after we broke up. And he had nothing to do with my ex-boyfriend. That was the first time I experienced how blind love makes you and how it gets you to forget about all the sensible red lines you promised never to cross. How ironic, right? But I had no control over the situation at all; nature's elements took over, leaving me at his mercy.

How did we meet? I met a mutual friend at a party only a few days before our encounter, so it was all unexpected. I started dating this friend, but nothing serious.

How did we fall in love? This friend and I rang the doorbell, and Dean opened it and smiled. I was hooked. It's as simple as that. And it was the first time I felt anything like that, as if a lightning bolt had hit me, and, which is even more strange, Dean felt it too. At least, that's what he pretended. I was screwed, standing there next to his friend while I was in love with him for no apparent reason other than a magical spell. At first, I did what I could not for it to show, not staring at him like a stupid, stupid bird. I always considered myself an intelligent girl, so I couldn't possibly give in to such a baseless feeling. I didn't even know anything about him, and for the control freak that I had become after what happened when I was fifteen, this was unimaginable. There was no way I would give in to it, period.

Who was I kidding? I would be the first teenager in history to resist love at first sight. It's the stuff fairy tales are made of, the ones every teen dreams about. But not me; I didn't want to lose all control in just a split second after looking at someone's smile. Unfortunately, I couldn't resist either. Every time we got together, because of his friend, we were like magnets, and our first kiss almost happened while his friend was present. Does this sound like a fairy tale? No, it sounds like hell, a sadistic spell. But I had no choice but to give in and live it, hoping to get through in one piece.

Dean became "my first."

After what happened when I was fifteen, I promised myself I would wait to be in a steady relationship with someone I loved before I gave myself to him. And it happened on the night before my seventeenth birthday. I believed I had the maturity required to understand the importance of that step in my life, and we were in our "honeymoon phase." On paper, I respected my promise, but in reality, I had a hard time coping with the physical part of it.

Our first time together was okay, but as our physical relationship developed, I experienced triggers for the first time. I tried my best to keep it hidden from him and to enjoy myself, but I rarely did. But when I couldn't hide it any longer and would cry out and roll into a fetal position, I wouldn't get any comfort or understanding from his end. He would just walk away and leave me there until it passed.

> *My senior year was the pinnacle of loneliness.*

Right before the start of my senior year, I moved in with him into a one-bedroom apartment that was big enough for the both of us. I would turn eighteen that coming November, so I took this opportunity to leave home. Little did I know I was trading one toxic environment for another, but at the time, any place seemed like a better option to me than my parents' home. I don't recall him ever inviting me to move in with him, but Dean never said he didn't want me to, either. Initially, I was only going to stay over for one night, but one night turned into two, then three, and so on, until I didn't go home. Nobody came searching for me or made any attempts to get me home, so I assumed they didn't mind either. What a shocker.

Dean had left school the previous academic year, so now he worked full-time while I was still attending school.

I found myself reliving my childhood experience, as, back then, I missed my father, and now I had to wait for my boyfriend to get home from work. Our hours didn't match well, as I had to get up early in the morning, study in the evening, and go to bed at a reasonable time. Dean slept in, went to work late in the morning, and worked well over midnight six days out of seven. He was enjoying his newfound freedom from school life and didn't have any respect for mine. Dean knew about my abandonment trauma and the fact that I had trouble sleeping alone in that apartment, which was located in the busy city center.

I asked him to please keep me informed about his plans after work if he wasn't coming home right away. That way, at least I wouldn't stay up waiting for him and could turn in and try to sleep. But no, he didn't share his plans, and I spent many nights crying because he acted as if I didn't exist in his life. The elevator was right next to our bedroom (how ironic), and I could hear it when it moved up and down. We were on the top floor (again), and I would follow the sound of the elevator moving while it came past every floor until it arrived at our level. Then I would hold my breath, hoping to hear him enter his key into the lock and open our front door. But that solace never came as soon as I would have liked. I feel so pitiful reminiscing about those nights and how helpless I was.

Going to school the next day, my eyes would be all puffy from the excessive crying. Even the best concealer couldn't mask it, but nobody ever asked me anything about it, not the students or the teachers. I was a shadow of who I used to be; being with him sucked all the remaining life out of me, and I have never felt lonelier than I did back then. I had no friends to confide in, no hobby or distraction to turn to; I just relied on him. As I turned eighteen, the school allowed me to get outside its walls for lunch. While most students went to the nearby café or park to eat, I hid behind a building. I sat on a windowsill where no one could see me and ate my sandwich alone— senior year, which I had always imagined being a yearlong party toward adult life, turned out to be the pinnacle of loneliness for me. What a shame; I think, looking back, I might have been depressed, as I was stuck in a sentiment I couldn't get out of. Yet, mental health issues weren't as known back then as they are now.

Her words still resonated in my mind.

I often thought, what the hell happened to me in that period? Even in the darkest times, I had always remained an independent girl, looking after myself and holding on to the possibilities of what the future might bring. Every time I fell down, I never stayed down for long. I would always pick myself back up and go on with my life. Even when I was living in fear, I still lived, so what happened to me now? What made me so weak and helpless? Her words happened; yes, the same toxic words Ursula had told me my entire childhood kept spreading through my body like venom, and it eventually poisoned my mind.

The physical abuse I endured as a child was brutal. It made me so sad and angry. But they didn't leave marks; they only lasted a moment, and when she stopped when I became a teenager, they just became a distant memory. But words are vicious; on paper, they sound less harmful than actual acts of physical violence. However, those words will remain with you forever. You may do your best to keep them hidden in some drawer, but eventually, they will reemerge and unleash their toxins to harm you.

As long as it was only me, her words didn't get through to me. When she said those words on a frequent basis, I was too young, and their content was still abstract to me. But after I grew into a young adult and found love, I became vulnerable to her "prophecies," such as: "You'll never achieve anything in your life"; "You're so hideous, and nobody cares about you"; and "You're just a stupid little girl." I could hear Ursula's voice resonate in my mind, especially when I was feeling down and insecure. I got stuck in a thought loop between her words and his.

Every time Dean said nasty things to me, her words became heavier, making it impossible for me to ignore them. I couldn't do anything to get them out of my head, and his wrong actions only worsened the situation, leaving me powerless to handle it with clarity. I was nothing more than a remnant of my former fighting self, who kept her power to go on even in the most desolate situations.

What a pity for me to be eighteen, in the physical prime of my life, graduating from high school in this disastrous state of mind. But that was my reality, and I can't change the past as much as I would want to. I had no special birthday party. I had no graduation party; those meaningful events just occurred as if it were any other day. And I feel sorry for my younger self, as I deserved more. It might have helped me through that "moment" when I got stuck mentally. But as I graduated high school in June of 2000, I was just a sad, unwanted girl.

I loved the movie *Pretty Woman*, and whenever I would watch the end scene where Richard Gere comes to save Julia Roberts, I always dreamt of being saved myself. And I was convinced I needed someone to love me in order to save me and to have a better life. Soon, I became codependent on my partner; I changed myself to match his needs and wishes out of fear of losing him. From the messed up example I had at home growing up, I thought it was normal for my partner to hurt me. And with Ursula's words running through my mind, I was living in an anxious state all the time.

It took me time to realize that love wouldn't come to save me and that my idea of love was off. If I had known then what I know now, I would have spared myself many broken hearts. That's why I'll share some of my relationships with you as a cautionary tale. Don't be fooled like I was; recognize specific patterns and walk out of there as soon as you can.

> We women need to support each other, right?
> And I've got your back.

What is love?

Love is care.
Love is support.
Love is being there.

Love is faith.
To love is to nourish.
To love is to cherish.

Love is pure.

To love others,
you must first learn
to love yourself.

Love is kind.
Love is real.

Love is life.

Take care of yourself,
inside and out.

A YOUNG WOMAN CRAVING LOVE

La syndrome della crocerossina

La syndrome della crocerossina is Italian for "Red Cross Syndrome," which means you're vulnerable to people with personal issues and are convinced you can save them or make them better. I suffered from this syndrome for more than a decade; I couldn't fight it. You could put twenty men in a room, and I would pick the most troubled ones out every time. From the outside, they were all made from the same mold: I always fell for the "bad boy" type, the ones who were rebellious, anti-conformist, morally gray, and appealing, of course.

I can't say I was alone in those love stories, as my partners made me believe they wanted to change. I didn't create this in my mind, but my convincement to be able to change them for the better was on me. What does it imply? You make excuses for their behavior, and you refuse to abandon them. You give it your all but get nothing in return. No matter what I did during the relationship, how hard I tried, or how much I loved them, I would end up alone and shattered. And if I can help even just one person recognize those aspects before getting hurt, it will be worth sharing this with the world.

These are three of my most important love stories; they kept me going for about three years each and left me heartbroken. I will share some hurtful events and missed red flags for you to relate to. Having an objective view of things is hard when you're neck-deep in it and blinded by your feelings. This is my way of showing my solidarity with others who might find themselves in a similar relationship or will be in the future. Not all types of abuse are visible from the outside or leave marks on your skin. The scars that people endure in toxic relationships are often invisible, but they last forever.

Psychological abuse: humiliation

Back story

Dean was my high school boyfriend, whom I told you about in the last chapter. I've already told you the story of how we met and how I felt it was love at first sight. That type of attraction made it even harder for me because I didn't have any choice in the matter or even know anything about him, and yet I still felt I was head over heels in love with someone I didn't even know.

The silent treatment

One of his weapons to punish me was the silent treatment, and for someone who felt invisible to her own family, this was absolute torture. Every time, it drove me mad until I begged him to stop. When Dean used it, he had total power over me, as I felt desperate for him to stop and give me some attention.

I remember one episode that hurt me to the core; we were walking back to his place after spending time at a café with some friends. And suddenly, Dean shoved me so hard that I fell off the sidewalk and landed on the street. If a car or a motorcycle had passed at that moment, they would have hit me. I was oblivious to why he acted that way; I was shocked and just sat there on the border for a bit. He didn't look back even for a second; I watched him walk away as if nothing had happened, waiting for him to turn around. But he never did.

I was confused and unsure of what to do, so after a while, I just got back up and walked to his place. When I arrived, his door was still open, and Dean was preparing to go to work. He never even acknowledged I was there; he just kept preparing to go to work without saying a thing, without even looking at me. I was utterly lost; I didn't know what to say or what to do, so I just stood there waiting for an absolution that would never come. He finished preparing and left just like that.

That triggered a violent reaction in me; since I was very much like a dormant volcano, the built-up tension suddenly released like a destructive explosion. I wanted to scream it out and yell out to the world that I was not invisible. I was crying out all the frustration his behavior had unleashed, as I had done nothing to deserve how he treated me. That's when I noticed some bottles of beer that Dean drank earlier, and my resentment grew, as alcohol certainly didn't improve his behavior. On the contrary, any addictive substance would only make them worse, but that didn't stop him from using those substances.

As my rage grew, I took those bottles one by one and threw them against the kitchen wall. Seeing them shatter into pieces felt good, so I kept doing it until I broke them all. As I let myself fall on the floor, I saw a piece of glass next to me. I don't know what came over me as I took it and began to rub it against my hand, trying to harm myself. In some ways, I was facing similar emotions to what I had experienced in my darkest time when I was fifteen. Maybe I wanted to punish myself for being in that situation, as a part of me felt guilty, just as I had back then. I should have been smarter than that. I should have known better.

Even in my anger and distress, I could see the gravity of what I was doing and made myself stop. I realized then and there that I was out of myself and needed help. I picked myself up again and ran to a nearby phone booth (no cell phones yet at that time), and I called him at work, telling him what I had done. Dean came back, and a part of me was glad he did, as it showed some love toward me. However, a few minutes later, the doorbell rang; he had called my parents before coming over. I felt betrayed that he had called my parents. It felt like he was handing me over to an executioner.

I remember looking at him with disbelief and looking at them with frustration. I stood there halfway between both parties on the threshold. Nobody was talking; they were just staring at me as if I were a bomb that needed to be dismantled. I could even see commiseration in their expressions, as if I were a lunatic that needed to wear a straitjacket. And that made me so mad. I wanted to scream, "You're the reason I became like this; you all are!" How hypocritical of them to stand there as if they could ever be a source of help for me. They messed me up, and I mean both parties. Ursula had started her work of destruction long ago, and Dean appeared to have come to finish it.

I never knew why he did what he did that day, and the reason doesn't matter; it's the perfect example of how someone can misbehave without any fault of our own. Why would he ever take responsibility for any of his actions when blaming other people was so much easier? It was never his fault, and he was always provoked by others. Convenient, right? And I appeared to be his chosen "cause" during our relationship.

Words as dangerous as sharp knives

When I left home at seventeen, I hoped I had left the psychological abuse behind me. But no, Dean liked to use words to hurt me too. He didn't do it at first; it was a weapon he kept hidden for about the first year of our relationship. But once he took it out, it only got easier for him to use, as if he enjoyed seeing what it did to me. And maybe diminishing me made him feel better about himself

One of the worst things Dean ever said to me was: "You're worth less than the crap sticking to my shoes." Wow, that hurt! I still remember the scene after almost thirty years, so if he wanted to make a lasting impression, he accomplished that. That kind of brutality left me speechless; I didn't know how to respond to that, as he had just stabbed me in the heart. What could his reasoning have been, other than complete humiliation? Making me feel worthless?

A phrase Dean used to say a lot was, "You're lucky for me to love you; who would ever love you if I didn't?" The worst thing was that it resonated as truth with what Ursula used to say to me. It was like simple math: one plus one equals two. So, that particular phrase would aggravate my codependency more than anything. It made me think that he was right, that I was lucky to have him, and I was even more scared of losing him.

But the most hurtful thing Dean dared to say to me once was that he doubted if what I told him about my first time at fifteen was the truth. I think he was fed up with my triggers and not being the sex addict he really wanted. But nothing justifies him saying that and meaning it too. How low can you go? What did I have to gain by making something like that up? He was worse to me. Whenever I suffered from acute triggers, I would push him away. So then, why would I make this up and fake this? He just wanted to crush my soul; that's what I think. And if I remember his words after all these years, he did an excellent job at it.

A new horizon

I've always been a proud nerd, I must add, as I'm a forever learner. Since I was little, I've always been curious about many things. Always questioning and trying to understand how things work and what purpose they serve. So, after graduating from high school, I went to college to improve my knowledge of foreign languages. Even though I lived in a city renowned for its universities, with students from all over the world, I decided to commute to the nation's capital. I wanted a change of scenery, to get to know new people and expand my horizons.

At that same time, Dean decided to leave his job and

go back to school to get his high school degree, a choice I supported. But it put us on different roads, adding tension and misunderstandings to our fragile relationship. But one specific incident would put the first nail in our relationship's coffin. It was December of my first year, and I returned home in the early evening; it was dark and cold outside, so I was eager to get inside and get some rest. As I went to unlock the front door, my key didn't turn. Even after several trials, it didn't budge, meaning he was home, and his key was on the inside. So I knocked on the door, rang the bell, and called him on his phone, but nothing happened. I could hear that the television was on, but nothing else.

Frustration was rising within me, as I could only imagine the state Dean was in, not to hear me making all that noise. Living in an apartment building, I tried not to make too much noise to alarm the neighbors. While sitting on the stairway, I felt humiliated, waiting for him to wake up and open the door. Waiting for about two or three hours, banging on the door and ringing the bell every few minutes. I felt like crying, like shouting; and kept thinking about how I had ended up in such an absurd situation and how it was uncalled for that he was treating me this way. Once again, he lived his life as if he were single and did not care about me at all.

Finally, on one of my attempts, Dean opened the door, looking mad at me as he woke up from sleeping off his hangover. Since he'd gone back to high school, he was behaving like a teenager again, so on the last day of his exams, he went out for drinks with his classmates and got wasted. He was acting as if he couldn't care less about the one he was supposed to love and care for. And when he opened the door, he looked dreadful and annoyed. Imagine me, after a long stressful day, having to wait about two hours on the stairway for him to wake up and open the door so I could get in.

This time, I was fed up with his irresponsible and uncaring behavior. I wanted to express how I felt, how mad and frustrated I was, but Dean wasn't interested in hearing about it. But I couldn't let it go. It was the first time in two years of a relationship that I stood up for myself, and it felt liberating. He had put me through enough already; this time, he would hear me out. He pushed me against the wall as I stood in his way. That was the last straw for me. I accepted many things, but physical violence was a deal-breaker for me.

I felt empowered.

After Dean pushed me, I grabbed my bag, filled it with some clothes and personal things, and left. So I took the bus and returned home, as it seemed to be the lesser of two evils at that time. I wasn't the frightened child anymore; I wasn't the clueless teen anymore. For the first time in years, I felt empowered and ready to take my life back. It felt like the time had come to put me first and think about my life. For the first time, Dean wasn't my first priority, which seemed impossible in our relationship.

Even though my parents didn't roll out the red carpet for me at home, they didn't keep me from returning either. My father was happy and relieved, as he was always worried about me living on my own at such a young age. Even if he never did anything to make me change my mind or return home. I never lived with my ex again, but it would still take over a year to get out of this "love at first sight spell" for good. It was a rollercoaster ride with some highs and far too many lows, break-ups, and getting back together until I was free for good in the spring of '02.

I told you those lightning strikes are the worst, based on natural elements you have no control over. You feel those intense feelings and are overwhelmed by them. The only advice I can give you is to recognize the behavior and the signs and understand it will only get worse. The key is to keep your eyes and ears open and get out of there as soon as you can.

Something for you to reflect on:

If someone asks about your relationship
and you lie about how it is,
then it's clearly not a healthy one.

If someone asks about your relationship
and you feel the need to hide certain aspects,
then it's clearly not a healthy one.

*If someone asks about your relationship
and you can't state at least five things you love about your partner,
then it's clearly not a healthy one.*

Playing hot and cold: mind games

Back story

I met him at the airport while waiting to board the flight back home from another summer in Italy. Vin was waiting in the same line, and since the plane needed maintenance, which delayed the flight, we got to talk. I always traveled alone, so I was glad to have someone to talk to for once. Once we got on the plane, I did something I never thought I would do: I impulsively asked my neighbor if he would mind changing his seat with him, and to my surprise, he immediately agreed. When I turned my head to tell him to join me, it was as if Vin was waiting for it. It's so weird; sometimes life seems to push you in a particular direction, and you go with the flow.

Vin stood up and smiled at me while he made his way through the pathway, and that's when it happened . . . again! I couldn't believe it either. I thought, *Come on, are you kidding me? Not again!* But just like the first time, I didn't have a say or choice, and this time, I was stuck sitting a few inches from him inside an airplane for over two hours. In such moments, I believe some cynical person is laughing their ass off, enjoying seeing me go through these incredible events.

The one who broke his heart

One of the first things Vin told me when we started dating was that he'd had one serious relationship, and she left him, never to return. That broke his heart, making it turn to stone. After enduring that heartbreak, Vin was incapable of falling in love again, and he didn't know who or what would be capable of making his heart beat again. No, I'm not making this up. This is not a scene from some romance I've read before; he had such a way of telling this story that I felt I wanted to take on the challenge of unfreezing his heart. Who knows how many times Vin had shared that same sobbing story with other women, convincing them to take on the same challenge.

Of course, his frozen heart still beat when Vin needed some physical attention; Vin had no problems in that department. On the contrary, our relationship turned out to be primarily physical, as that was the only interaction that made him feel things for someone else. That was a first for me, but maybe the only positive part of this relationship, as, for the first time, I could feel passion without experiencing triggers like I used to. Maybe because before, I felt forced to keep my ex satisfied? Because I couldn't say "no" to him for fear of losing him? I don't know, but I didn't feel pressured. Vin was eight years older than me; Vin was a "tortured soul," and he played hard to get, which was exciting. He knew what he was doing with his mind games, and I actually felt I was doing what I wanted for me and not for him. Chapeau! Nice game.

Vin wouldn't let me go.

Have you seen the romantic comedy *The Holiday* starring Cameron Diaz and Kate Winslet? If you have, you'll quickly understand the toxic issues in this relationship. If you haven't, follow my lead, as the situation is quite easy to explain. Kate Winslet's character is madly in love with her ex, Jasper Bloom, who never fully commits to her. But he always keeps an active role in her life, just for his personal benefit, making it impossible for her to get over him and move on. She can't move on, as he revives the flame by bringing up ancient memories of their relationship, and whenever he feels she is getting away, he shows up to wheel her back into his net.

Just as Jasper did in *The Holiday*, Vin was playing a mind game with me. Some would even call it a mindf*ck, as that incomprehensible behavior, playing hot and cold and sending mixed messages, was so confusing. It made me overthink twenty-four hours a day, obsessing about each word Vin said and every move he made. I included my girlfriends in my obsession with trying to decipher his behavior. Even the more experienced girls didn't have a clue. It was just cruelty disguised as a romance, and it was intriguing for a while, but in the long run, it was emotionally exhausting. Relationships like this are emotionally and physically draining when you're in love. If you don't have genuine feelings for the person, you could probably cope with it; however, when you're dreaming of a "happily ever after," you can't keep holding on to someone like this.

Whenever I thought to myself, *I'm done*, Vin had to make up his mind, or I would move on; Vin would play the victim. He would tell me how amazing I am and how lucky any guy would be to build a life with someone like me. But for some mysterious reason, he would add that he wasn't the one to provide that for me. His monologue made you want to fight more for him as you tried to help him find his way to love again. It took me about two years to be freed from this spell.

I remember the last time we kissed; I felt nothing and was so happy about that. So when I told him I didn't feel anything and could finally move on, Vin wasn't thrilled for me at all. Vin kept asking me for a retry, which I could refuse. Even after I left, Vin kept texting me, asking for another opportunity to kiss me, as he had given me a lousy goodbye kiss and could have done a lot better. And I remember smiling; for the first time, I saw through his game as he attempted to play me once again. It was clear to me it was all about his ego, never about me or my genuine feelings for him. Therefore, this time, I was done for real.

Something for you to reflect on:

*If they say someone would be lucky to have you,
but for whatever reason,
they can't give you what you need,
then they don't really love you.*

*If they say their heart was broken long ago,
and they need more time to commit,
then they don't really love you.*

*If they say they miss you, can't wait to see you,
but they never seem to have the time to meet,
then they don't really love you.*

Pathological liar: gaslighting

Back story

I met him while I was studying abroad. Pablo was charming and made me laugh. He might have been the first guy who seduced me, and not the other way around. Pablo made me feel desirable as a woman and knew how to draw my attention. This time, my sentiment grew little by little, which was so refreshing after being struck by lightning twice. The slow-paced beginning seemed promising, making me feel at ease and more in control.

Pablo gained my trust, as he seemed to be outspoken and bold. I confided in him; he wrote me letters expressing his feelings; it was all new to me. We were just two damaged yet strong-willed people who had a hunger for a better life and were eager to fulfill our dreams. His mother embraced me when I came into their lives; we even became friends, spending time together as women. I felt as if I had gained a new family, not just a romantic relationship. She trusted me and said I had a positive influence on her son, which was one of the best compliments I could receive. She perceived a change for the good, which made me happy, yet it also gave me responsibility. But I didn't mind; I wanted to help him get better.

As I was living by myself at the time, Pablo needed to move out of his place a few weeks into the relationship, and it made sense for him to move in with me—not only to save money but also to get to know each other better. This would be my second time living with someone, and I hoped it would be the last.

The missing earrings

One day, the earrings Pablo got me for Christmas went missing. I looked everywhere for them, but I couldn't find them. Therefore, I felt awful about it, and after a few days, I told him about it before he noticed I wasn't wearing them anymore. And I didn't want him to think I didn't care for them. When I told him, he got mad; he accused me of being careless with my belongings, and I felt terrible about losing his gift. I felt so sad; I apologized and said I was mortified. Even after searching everywhere, I still had no idea where they might be. Pablo added he was disappointed in me, which made me feel worse because I was anything but an irresponsible person.

A short while later, as I emptied his pockets to do his laundry, I found a piece of paper. As I opened it, I saw it was from a pound shop. Further down the paper, it said, "silver earrings," and the amount the shop paid for them. Man, I fell hard from my pink cloud at that moment. I couldn't believe Pablo would sell the earrings Pablo gifted me for a small amount of money. The worst thing was how he attacked me verbally when I told him I couldn't find them anymore. How could he have played me that well? I didn't have a clue; I didn't doubt him even a little. Pablo kept playing with my mind for days, expressing his disappointment in me. How could he fool me like that with a straight face?

I waited for him to come home and considered testing how far Pablo would take his little act. After he came home from work, I brought up the lost earrings again, saying how sad I was because I loved them. He said he never thought I could be so careless, yada yada, until I took out the receipt and confronted him. At first, Pablo even tried to deny knowing what that was, but when he saw I wouldn't take his crap, he started laughing. I mean, laughing out loud as if he had told a fabulous joke. It was like watching Dr. Jekyll turn into Mr. Hyde. He acted like it was no big deal, turned it into something silly, and told me not to worry about it.

Pablo faked going to work.

Being a recovering addict, it was challenging for him to find employers willing to give him a chance. But thanks to his charming character, Pablo would get some opportunities. Every day, he got up, went to work before me, and came home in the evening after me. I was proud of him;

the fact that he was trying to take his life back while doing a job he enjoyed was the cherry on top. We would share details about our days at work during dinner time, as all couples do. I would tell him something about my day, and he would do the same about his.

But the road to permanent recovery is tough, and people make mistakes sometimes. Eventually, Pablo relapsed, and the best way for him to get clean was to enter a recovery center for some time. It wasn't his first time there, so we already knew the staff and how it worked. Of course, I was anxious to find myself all alone again, responsible for all the bills, etc. But I supported his efforts to get clean again. Before he entered rehab, he asked me to go by his employer, as his boss still owed him for some hours. He said it would help me face some of the financial obligations.

So, one day after work, I drove to his employer. I went to his office, and he was kind enough to see me without an appointment. After some small talk, he added he was pretty surprised to see me there, seeing as how his collaboration with my partner had ended. I didn't know what he was talking about, so I explained that Pablo sent me to pick up some remaining pay. His eyes went wide, as if he had seen a ghost, and he said, "I don't know how to tell you this, but Pablo hasn't been to work for weeks." I felt as if I were the biggest fool in the universe. But why would Pablo send me there? Why would he put me in such a difficult position and make such a fool out of me? I felt so humiliated, and his employer felt terrible for me, as I started crying. As I walked out, I had to face all the pitiful looks on the other team members' faces. I just wanted to run out of there, but I kept it together as much as possible.

By then, Pablo was already inside the center, with no means for outside communication. I had no way to confront him, but in the end, what kind of plausible explanation could he give me? He became such a talented pathological liar that I don't know if he even knew what was true anymore. I was distraught, so I called his mom to confide in her, and she was mortified too. She didn't know what to tell me either, except to have faith in his new recovery and keep supporting him. Maybe this time, Pablo would change for real. A few weeks later, I received a letter from him, telling me how sorry he was for what he did and the lies he'd told me. He said he would do anything to improve it and build the life we always wanted together. I have a heart, and I'm not one to kick someone when they're down, so I waited for him to return.

"Honey, I'm out for cigs."

How many movies, cartoons, or series use this line in a scene to show how someone has somehow disappeared from their lives? Only in fiction, right? Wrong! It actually happened to me. But not to pick up cigarettes, Pablo left for work like any other day. We even took the train together; he took his performance that far, and I had no clue there would have been something of that particular morning. While I was setting up at my office, he called to ask me to notify his boss, as he was running a little late—so I sent his boss an email.

A few hours later, while I was at work, his boss called me, asking me to call him back as soon as I could. I worked in a call center, so I couldn't get off the phone as quickly as I would've liked; it was noon by the time I was able to call him back. His boss asked if I knew where Pablo was, as they were worried because he hadn't shown up for work yet.

Naturally, I got worried, too, so I called him, but the phone rang with no answer. As time passed, I was freaking out as I imagined horrible scenarios, including him being mugged, falling off the tracks at the station, or getting run over by a bus. I imagined it all, except the real truth behind his disappearance. That never even crossed my mind. I wrote to his parents and mutual friends, asking them to let me know if they had any news.

But then, after my lunch break, I received a message from his father, telling me Pablo had left the country. He had left the country and, therefore, *me*, period. Just like that, no explanation, no farewell, nothing at all. I felt like I was about to faint; we had been living together for over two years, and I had been by his side, supporting him through thick and thin. I stayed by him in his darkest hours; how could he ever do something like this to me? Why would he leave me this way, acting as if our relationship had never even existed at all? Who had I been with all this time? But that's exactly what he did.

Pablo faked his way through going to work that day.

He even faked his goodbye to me.

He had faked his commitment to us all along.

Because of his carelessness, a friendly colleague had to drive me home that evening. I was completely numb, empty, and oblivious, and I was in no emotional state to drive. This was another kind of heartache, one I had never felt before. It hurt me on so many levels.

In the end, Pablo did me a big favor, as I was far too loyal to leave him. If he had stayed, I might have continued indulging him in the name of love and support. The thing is, I was used to fighting and had been fighting for most of my life. But I didn't know when it was time to quit, to let go. It wasn't until a decade later that I finally mastered the fine art of letting go. I hope you won't have to wait that long and will learn that sometimes it's time to let go of the things that consume and hurt you. Letting go of unhealthy things is not a failure, as you're making a reasoned decision to go the other way because that's what you need to do for yourself. And you should.

Something for you to reflect on:

*If they accuse you of lying or cheating
but you're the one doubting their behavior,
then they're clearly lying to you.*

*If they deny any of your allegations
but you have proof of what you're stating,
then they're clearly lying to you.*

*If they tell you what you want to hear
but you know their words don't add up,
then they're clearly lying to you.*

True love
If you have to change yourself
to be with someone,
that means
it isn't love.
True love means
accepting your partner,
loving who they are
on the inside.
True love means
being free
to be you.
True love is rare;
be aware
of the fakes.

CONCLUSION

I believe people can change, but only if they want to. It must be their decision for it to be a lasting change. We can't force people to change; that doesn't work. Finding your "why" and having a solid purpose for change is essential.

> It's safe to say that I survived my childhood.
>
> It's safe to say that I had to fight from the day I was born.
>
> It's safe to say that I went through hell and came back around.

I have no superpowers; I'm just a woman who chose to live, to get back up again, and to believe in something good. Just because I had to go through it all alone, I believe nobody should ever have to do that.

> That's why I'm sharing my story.
> That's why I'm writing about my life.

I wish to support and empower you by showing you can still overcome, no matter what you have gone through.

Life can be challenging, but that doesn't make it impossible.

It's never too late to regain control over your life.

Don't ever feel guilty about what happened to you.
Don't ever keep negative events a secret for too long.
Don't ever punish yourself for what others did to you.

Your past is behind you.
Your past doesn't define you.
Your past is made of ashes, fertile soil you can rise from.

> I welcome you to follow me online, be motivated by my words, and reach out to me.
>
> All useful links are available on my website; you'll find my author page too:
>
> www.pacha1.be

Please let me know how you felt reading my story.

If you could relate to my words, if they gave you some comfort or motivation, be so kind as to leave a review. I would appreciate it, as I still need to grow and learn as an author.

If you appreciate my writing and want to read more, please have a look at my previous work, *Drops of life experience*, a motivational memoir that offers a unique look inside the mind of a fellow trauma survivor and chronic pain warrior—available in your favorite online stores.

> THIS BOOK IS DEDICATED TO ALL THE EMOTIONAL
> AND PHYSICAL TRAUMA SURVIVORS OUT THERE.
> YOU'RE NOT ALONE.

*As a trauma survivor,
it mattered to me,
acknowledging
my inner child's
pain and sorrow.
I'm so grateful to her
for holding on
without anyone
to help
or support her.
Alone,
no more.
Silent,
no longer.*

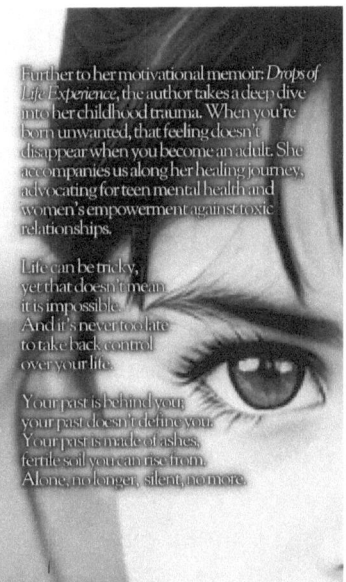

Further to her motivational memoir: *Drops of Life Experience*, the author takes a deep dive into her childhood trauma. When you're born unwanted, that feeling doesn't disappear when you become an adult. She accompanies us along her healing journey, advocating for teen mental health and women's empowerment against toxic relationships.

Life can be tricky,
yet that doesn't mean
it is impossible.
And it's never too late
to take back control
over your life.

Your past is behind you;
your past doesn't define you.
Your past is made of ashes,
fertile soil you can rise from.
Alone, no longer; silent, no more.

My purpose as a writer is to help, and motivate others.
I care and I understand because I'm one of you: a trauma survivor and a chronic illness/pain warrior.

Being an introverted, Highly sensitive mother, I'm quite empathetic.
You might even say I'm a sponge for emotions.

I'm a thought instigator who loves to make people think about everything.
A modern-day philosopher and sometimes poet.

My debut as an author is a motivational memoir, Drops of Life Experience, released last October.

I'm the proud mom of two teenage boys and I care for animals. We adopted nine pets over the years.

One of my credos is: "If you can't help everyone, just help one." No one should be left alone in this world. That counts for animals as well.

You have the power to change things.

Take care of yourself, inside and out.

www.ingramcontent.com/pod-product-compliance
Lightning Source LLC
LaVergne TN
LVHW041534070526
838199LV00046B/1658